the co-op principle
Hannes Meyer
and the Concept of
Collective Design

D1686017

Syd
Nick
Roger
Richard

collective 31

Exhibition catalogue published by Werner Möller in collaboration with Raquel Franklin for the Bauhaus Dessau Foundation

The project was realised

under the patronage of the Swiss Ambassador to the Federal Republic of Germany, H.E. Tim Guldimann

in cooperation with the Universidad Anáhuac México Norte, the programme "Bewegte Netze" (Bauhaus members and their contact networks in the 1930s and 1940s) of the German Research Foundation (DFG), Brandenburg University of Technology (BTU) Cottbus-Senftenberg, the Anhalt University of Applied Sciences, the Stadtarchiv Dessau-Roßlau, the Deutsche Werkstätten Hellerau and the Arbeits- und Sozialförderungsgesellschaft Dessau e.V.

with support from the Archives of the Deutsches Architekturmuseum in Frankfurt am Main, the Institut für Geschichte und Theorie der Architektur (gta) at the ETH Zürich, the Bauhaus-Archiv Berlin, the Bauhaus Dessau Foundation, the Siedlungsgenossenschaft Freidorf in Muttenz, BL, and the Kunstmuseum Olten

The project was funded

by the International Museum Fellowship Programme of the German Federal Cultural Foundation

KULTURSTIFTUNG
DES
BUNDES

and with sponsorship of the Swiss Arts Council Pro Helvetia and Lotto-Toto GmbH Sachsen-Anhalt.

Collective 32

Louis
Peter
Curly
Vince
Roger
Mushy
Anthony
Jimmy
Josh
Sam
Danny

Going Down

the co-op principle – Hannes Meyer and the Concept of Collective Design

Spector Books

Athos

Porthos

Aramis

d'Artagnan

Collectiv 33

Foreword

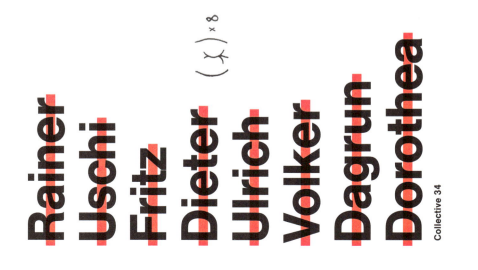

Exhibition
Curated by Raquel Franklin and Werner Möller

Themes

Satellites

Collective 35
Balthasar
Melchior
Caspar

Hannes Meyer's collective

Claudia Perren
Director and Chief Executive Officer
of the Bauhaus Dessau Foundation

2015 is the year of the collective at the Bauhaus Dessau Foundation. It deals with the masses and with class, with the relationship of the individual to society. From 1919 to 1933 the Bauhauslers saw themselves as members of a creative collective for learning, work and experimentation, in which they not only gave shape to the products and visions of a new way of living, but also put these to the test first-hand. The tenor and context of the collective concept changed several times over the 14-year history of the school, not least due to the different objectives of the directors Walter Gropius, Hannes Meyer and Mies van der Rohe: From the idea of an elitist visionary community to cooperative collective models through to liberal network concepts.

With the exhibition "The Co-op Principle – Hannes Meyer and the Concept of Collective Design", the Foundation takes an in-depth look at the design practice of the second Bauhaus director for the first time. With his appointment in 1928, Hannes Meyer brought about a change of thinking: From the author-architect to the office collective, from the need for luxury to the needs of the people. With regard to the composition of his collective, it was believed that the more varied the competencies of the collaborators, the more effective the team and the more worthwhile the results. His concept of the collective was not about harmony, uniformity or even stylistic orientation, but about the methodological approach of diverse specialists with the objective of integrating as many factors as possible in the architectonic design process. His building

Pages 8/9: The legendary Metal Party at the Bauhaus Dessau with its director Hannes Meyer, carnival, 9.2.1929, photo attributed to Walter Funkat

programmes were to evolve from scientifically founded analytical processes. He worked with charts and diagrams, analysed psychological and functional aspects and their economic and societal consequences. And although the buildings of his office collective have a specific aesthetic, for Hannes Meyer architecture is not an aesthetic process, but above all an organisation of the analysed factors.

With the introduction of vertical brigades, Hannes Meyer likewise pursues the objective of interdisciplinary work in the collective in lessons. For him, design becomes the link between individual and society. He also favours working with the students on real, rather than hypothetical, building projects. Especially in his time at the Bauhaus it becomes evident that his vision of modernism is directed at a broad spectrum of the population. He calls for "new standards" for the "new people" of a "new world". He achieves his aim of creating decent housing with the same level of comfort for everyone with the construction of 90 apartments in the balcony access houses in Dessau-Törten and in the 'Volkswohnung'. In all this, his approach is characterised by the conviction that the collective serves the design process. For the Bauhaus Dessau Foundation, this principle provides not only the substance for historical reflection, but also the background and reason for inquiry into the contemporary possibilities and potentials of collective design.

bauhaus and society

in every creative design appropriate to living
we recognise
an organised form of existence.
given proper embodiment
every creative design appropriate to living is
a reflection of contemporary society. –
building and design are for us one and the same,
and they are a social process.
as a 'university of design'
the dessau bauhaus is not an artistic,
but a social phenomenon.

as creative designers
our activities are determined by society,
and the scope of our tasks is set by society.
does not our present society in Germany call for thousands
of people's schools, people's parks, people's houses?
hundred of thousands of people's flats??
millions of pieces of people's furniture???
(what are the connoisseurs' gibberings worth when set
against these)
(after the cubistic cubes of bauhaus objectivity?)
thus we take the structure and the vital needs
of our community as given.
we seek to achieve
the widest possible survey of the people's life,
the deepest possible insight into the people's soul,
the broadest possible knowledge of this community.
as creative designers
we are servants of this community.
our work is a service to the people.

all life is an urge towards harmony.
growing means
striving after the harmonious enjoyment of
oxygen + carbon + sugar + starch + protein.
work means
our search for the harmonious form of existence.
we are not seeking
a bauhaus style or a bauhaus fashion.
no modishly-flat plane-surface ornamentation
divided horizontally and vertically and all done up in neo-
plastic style.
we are not seeking
geometric or stereometric constructions,
alien to life and inimical to function.
we are not in Timbuctoo:
ritual and hierarchy
are not dictators of our creative designing.
we despise every form
which is prostituted into a formula.
thus the aim of all bauhaus work is
to bring together all vitally creative forces
so as to give harmonious shape to our society.

as members of the bauhaus we are seekers:
we seek the harmonious work,
the outcome of the conscious organisation
of intellectual and spiritual forces.
every human work is target-oriented
and the world of its creator is apparent in it.
this is the creator's life-line.
thus our work
collective in aim and embracing the broad masses in its scope
becomes a manifestation of the philosophy of life.

"Photo through the co-op display window", Natalie
Meyer-Herkert photographed by Hannes Meyer, n.y.,
from the quarterly "bauhaus. vierteljahr-zeitschrift
für gestaltung" year 3 (1929) issue 1, p. 3

art?!
all art is organisation.
the organisation of the dialogue
between this world and the other,
the organisation of sense impressions of the human eye,
and accordingly subjective, bound to the person,
and accordingly objective, determined by society.
art is not a beauty aid, art is not a discharge of affect,
art is only organisation.

classical:
in the module of the logical geometry of Euclid,
gothic:
in the acute angle as the pattern of passion,
renaissance:
in the golden section as the rule of balance.
art has always been nothing but organisation.
we of today long to obtain through art solely
the knowledge of a new objective organisation,
meant for all,
manifesto and mediator of a collective society.
thus a
theory of art
becomes a system of organising principles
and indispensible to every creative designer.
thus
being an artist is no longer a profession
but the vocation to become a creator of order.
thus
bauhaus art is also a means of experimenting
in objective order.

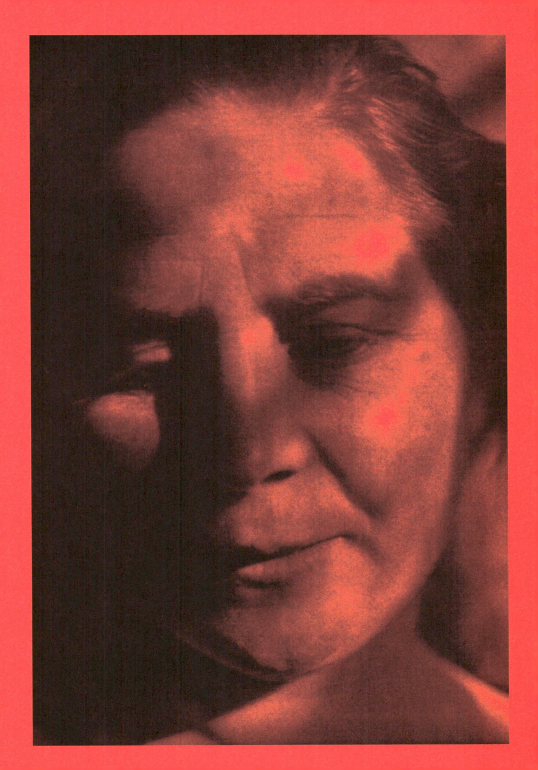

the new building school
as a center of education in shaping life
makes no selection of the gifted.
it despises
the imitative intellectual mobility of talent,
it is alive to the danger of intellectual schism:
inbreeding, egocentrism, unworldliness, aloofness.
the new building school
is a checkpoint for testing aptitude.
somewhere someone has an aptitude for something.
life refuses no one.
a capacity for symbiosis
is inherent in every individual.
hence education for creative design engages
the whole man.
removes inhibitions, anxiety, repression.
eliminates pretense, bias, prejudice.
it unites the liberation of the designer
with the capacity
for becoming identified with society.

the new theory of building
is an epistemology of existence.
as a theory of design
it is the song of songs of harmony.
as a theory of society
it is a strategy for balancing
co-operative forces and individual forces
within the community of a people.
this theory of building is not a theory of style.
it is not a constructivist system,
it is not a doctrine of technical miracles.
it is a system for organising life,
and it likewise clarifies

physical, psychical, material, and economic concerns.
it explores, delimits, and orders the fields of force
of the individual, the family, and society.
its basis is the recognition of the living space
and the knowledge of the periodicity of the process of living.
spiritual distance is as important to it
as the distance measured in metres.
its creative media are – deliberately employed –
the results of biological research.
because this doctrine of building is close to life's realities
its theses are constantly changing:
because it finds concrete existence in life,
its forms are as rich in content
as life itself.
'richness is all.'

finally all creative action is determined by the fate
of the landscape
which is unique and unparalleled for the one settled down
the work being personal and localised.
if a moving population lacks this native land
its work easily becomes stereotyped and standardised.
a conscious experience of the landscape
is building as determined by fate.
as creators we fulfill the fate of the landscape.

hannes meyer.

Hannes Meyer's "bauhaus and society" (1929)
From Hannes Meyer, Buildings, Projects, and Writings,
(Teufen AR/Schweiz. Arthur Niggli Ltd.: 1965).
Translated from the German by D.Q. Stephenson.

The Exhibition – The Themes – The Design

Werner Möller
Research Associate

Hannes Meyer's political commitment to Marxism and Stalinist Russia also influenced the reception of his work and con-
tributed significantly to his marginalisation as a figure alongside the two other Bauhaus directors, Walter Gropius and
Ludwig Mies van der Rohe. It was to take until 1965 – eleven
years after Meyer's death – before Claudia Schnaidt released
the first comprehensive monograph, ironically enough enhanced with an epilogue by the publisher, in which Walter
Gropius once again testily settled the score with his succes-
sor at the Bauhaus. Only in 1989, on what would have been
his 100th birthday, was it possible to dedicate a comprehensive exhibition to Hannes Meyer from an objective distance.
This was shown in Berlin, Frankfurt am Main, Zurich and
Dessau.

While this exhibition progressed chronologically through the
entire breadth of his creative oeuvre, the exhibition "The
Co-op Principle – Hannes Meyer and the Concept of Collective Design" focuses thematically on his practice of design.
Based on a considered selection of projects, the exhibition
conveys Hannes Meyer's understanding of a cooperative
design process: For him, it was a process that collectively
addressed broad sections of the population and, at the same
time, embodied "ideological protest" (Hannes Meyer, 1929).

Against the backdrop of Heinrich Pestalozzi's philosophy,
Meyer sought tangible, harmonious links between the individual and society through design, enhanced by the concept of
landscape as an element that determined fate. Based on

The Volkswohnung (People's flat) of the Bauhaus
Dessau exhibited in the Grassi Museum Leipzig,
1929, photo: Walter Peterhans

these references to Pestalozzi and the landscape, the exhibition is divided into four themes: Society, Education, Architecture and Landscape. The pertinent collective and cooperative projects and documents are allocated to each of these. In many of the projects, the themes intersect; the latter are therefore not self-contained, but overlap and thereby consistently reveal new cross-references. In this way the four themes form an exhibition landscape and illustrate Hannes Meyer's overarching cosmos of "ideological protest". The projects and themes likewise provide access to Meyer's diverse places of work in Switzerland, Germany, Russia and Mexico. Hannes Meyer's biographical networks are inextricably linked with these international migration paths. The exhibition will address aspects of his personal networks by way of example.

The touring exhibition of the Bauhaus Dessau in Kunstmuseum Basel, 1929, exhibition design by Hannes Meyer, photographer unknown

The touring exhibition of the Bauhaus Dessau in Kunsthalle Mannheim, 1930, exhibition design by Alfred Arndt, photographer unknown

In a separate studio, so-called satellites delineate the cosmos of Hannes Meyer under the following headings: Influences, ABC – Hannes Meyer and the Avant-garde, Politics and Migration, and Reception and Marginalisation. Employing a different perspective from the four main themes, they provide insights into the history of his development and impact. Reconstructions of furniture from the 'Volkswohnung' exhibition are integrated in the satellites as visual displays for public use. Although Meyer's time at the Bauhaus was so short-lived, the 'Volkswohnung' was entirely pivotal to his oeuvre. The trade fair-esque travelling exhibition of the Bauhaus of 1929/30, with products from the Bauhaus workshops, was closely linked with the concept of the 'Volkswohnung'. The exceptionally purist, precise and economical design of this presentation delivers the spatial and graphic reference for the exhibition "The Co-op Principle – Hannes Meyer and the Concept of Collective Design".

The central object

Designed in 1928 and completed in 1930, the school of the ADGB (Federation of German Trade Unions) in Bernau by Berlin is the most important work in Meyer's oeuvre, in which his cooperative design ideals and the four themes of the exhibition – society, education, architecture and landscape – culminate.

21

Hannes Meyer and Hans Wittwer with the
assistance of the Bauhaus Dessau, school of
the ADGB (Federation of German Trade Unions)
in Bernau by Berlin, 1928–1930,
photo: aerial photo by Junkers

Influences

Hannes Meyer's design practice is inextricably linked with both his family background and social origins. Born in 1889 the son of an architect in a well-established family in Basel, a twist of fate meant that he spent several years in an orphanage as a child. In the years thereafter, up until the end of WWI, he was shaped by the social crises in Switzerland and Germany and the land reform movements led by Johann Friedrich Schär und Adolf Damaschke that they inspired.

In this environment, Meyer found his way to the pedagogical philosophy of Johann Heinrich Pestalozzi. Its arrangement of individual and social life-nexus in five concentric circles and the relationships between personal and material environment derived therefrom had a huge influence on Meyer. Floor plans such as those for Dessau-Törten or Mümliswil, right up to the planning of satellite towns in Russia, show evidence of these influences. Likewise, the vertical brigades in Meyer's lessons at the Bauhaus reflect Pestalozzi's view that everyone has an inherent talent that is capable of development. Within these influences, the young Meyer delivered key insights for the economic and ergonomic questions of the innovative Swiss businessman and inventor Konrad von Meyenburg.

einige genossenschaftliche prinzipien

erstes prinzip.

die individualkraft

die kooperative kraft

gemeinkraft (Komponente)

jedes reale werk ist resultat geistiger voraussetzungen.
z. b. jedes haus ist als bauwerk die komponente diger 2 kräfte
dies ist das kriterium aller moderner architektur.

organisationsprinzip

A.G.V.

1. prinzip des grossen kreises
expansion nach aussen.
schlagen der jahresringe.
centralismus.

2. assoziation kleiner kreise.
um einen intensiven
kern. sog. zellensystem
(im städtebau satelitsystem)
trabantensystem.

2.a. gleichwertige zellen
an einer
gemeinsamen
linie

3 grundlagen menschlicher existenz

essen
arbeiten
wohnen.

1. genossenschaftlicher warenbezug = reine bedarfsdeckung.
das prinzip: rückvergütung im verhältnis zum warenbezug
keine dividende " " " kapital.
barzahlung.

2. bildung sozialen kapitals
durch organisation der sparkraft
(nicht durch spekulative gewinne oder profite.)
gemeinsamer besitz der produktionsmittel etc.

3. genossenschaftliche produktion.
reine bedarfswirtschaftliche erzeugung
(keine künstliche fabrikation mit spekulationsabsichten)

Hannes Meyer, planning for the co-operative
housing estate Freidorf above the Schänzli area
on the outskirts of Muttenz, Basel, 1920

Society

Hannes Meyer was active in the land reform and cooperative movements in Germany and Switzerland even before the First World War. These sought to strike a balance between capitalism and communism in favour of improved and more equitable provisions for the people.

In this context, in 1919 he joined the Verband Schweizerischer Konsumvereine (Association of Swiss consumer societies) and in the same year won the competition to design its first cooperative housing estate Freidorf in Muttenz, BL. With a centrally located "community house" and an own currency, the spatial and economic organisation exemplify the housing cooperative's autonomy. Meyer lived in Freidorf until 1926 and actively participated in propaganda for the cooperative, for example with the "Theater Co-op".

Having become acquainted with the Swiss avant-garde milieu, Meyer strove to "scientise" and internationalise his activities in design, with the aim of shaping a "new world". In this respect, the 1926 competition for the League of Nations building in Geneva arrived at just the right time: The League of Nations had just been founded; its idea and the building project were without precedent and infinitely international. Hannes Meyer and Hans Wittwer's office collective in Basel won one of the third prizes with its modern, avant-garde design. This brought Meyer his international breakthrough as an architect and his "admission ticket" for the Bauhaus.

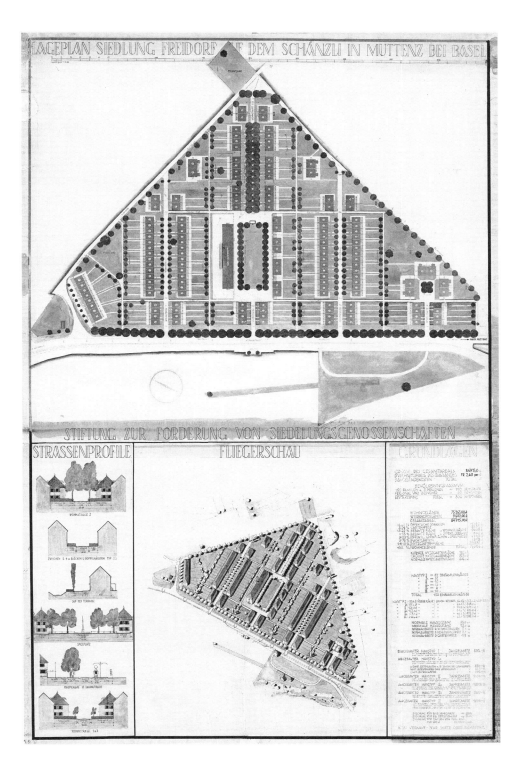

Fritz Zbinden, "Die Selbstverwaltung" (Self-government), one of 12 pages of cartoons on the life and organisation of the cooperative housing estate Freidorf, 1924. The pages were also part of the Theater Co-op production

"Co-operation rules the word.
The community rules the individual."

From: Hannes Meyer, DIE NEUE WELT, 1926

Hannes Meyer, street view of house type IIb on the co-operative housing estate Freidorf, 1921, photo: Theodor Hoffmann

Hannes Meyer, the community building of the co-operative housing estate Freidorf, 1924, photo: Theodor Hoffmann

Aerial photo of the co-operative housing estate Freidorf, post-1924

Hannes Meyer, elevations, cross sections and
floor plans of the community building of the
co-operative housing estate Freidorf, 1924

Hannes Meyer, interior view of the shop in
Freidorf, ca. 1924, photographer unknown

Hannes Meyer, untitled, abstract architecture II,
linocut, 1925/26. Isometric, constructivist graphic
rendering of an illustration of the shop in Freidorf

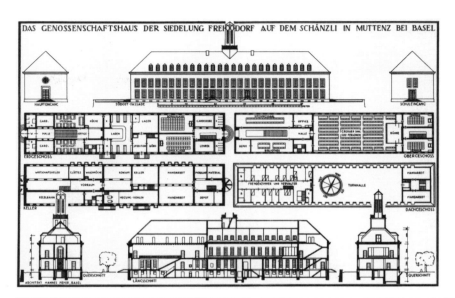

The community building combined all the main functions of
the housing co-operative. Arieh Sharon's notes for lessons at
the Bauhaus Dessau document the difference between the
co-op shop in Freidorf and a conventional small retail outlet.

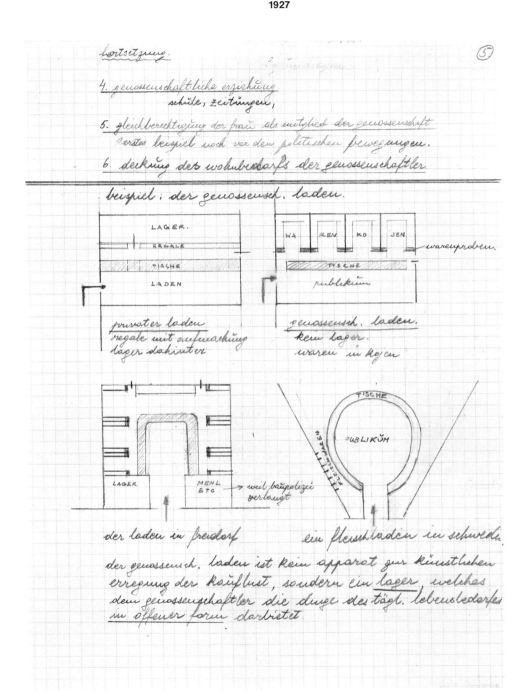

29

Arieh Sharon, notes from the class "The Cooperative" with Hannes Meyer at the Bauhaus Dessau,
1927

fortsetzung.   ⑤

4. genossenschaftliche erziehung
      schule, zeitungen,

5. gleichberechtigung der frau als mitglied der genossenschaft
      erstes beispiel noch vor den politischen bewegungen.

6. deckung des wohnbedarfs der genossenschaftler

beispiel : der genossensch. laden.

LAGER.
REGALE
TISCHE
LADEN

| WA | REN | KO | JEN | → warenproben. |
| TISCHE |
| publikum |

privater laden   genossensch. laden.
regale mit aufmachung   kein lager.
lager dahinter   waren in kojen

| LAGER | MEHL ETC | → weil baupolizei verlangt |

TISCHE
PUBLIKUM
FRISCHWAREN

der laden in freidorf   ein fleischladen in schwed.

der genossensch. laden ist kein apparat zur künstlichen
erregung der kauflust, sondern ein lager, welches
dem genossenschaftler die dinge des tägl. lebensbedarfes
in offener form darbietet.

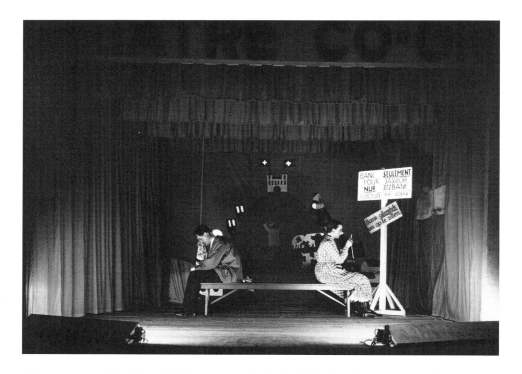

"How should it be? What could it be? It had to concede to tough conditions: Simplicity of plot and scenery, lighting and technical set-up. Omission of the word in deference to the bilingual Belgian population and the international exhibition visitors. More importantly, the necessity of describing the idea of the collective, to let its content be known, prove its benefit, with limited stage devices and no words".

From the leaflet "Theatre Co-op", Freidorf, 1924

Company of Jean Bard and Hannes Meyer, scenes
from performances of the propaganda play
Theater Co-op, Ghent and Freidorf, 1924. The
married couple Jean-Bard appeared as actors,
with Hannes Meyer as puppet master

Hannes Meyer, co-op display window design with products of the Swiss consumer co-operative society, Freidorf, 1925, photo: Theodor Hoffmann

Hannes Meyer, untitled, abstract architecture I, linocut, 1925/26. Rendering of the co-op display window in constructivist graphics

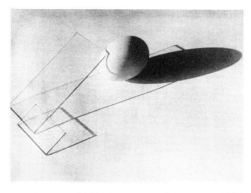

Hannes Meyer, "Co-op. Construction", photo, 1926, photo: Hannes Meyer

Hannes Meyer, untitled, graphic construction I, linocut, 1925/26

Hannes Meyer, "DIE WOHNUNG Co-op. Interieur 1926" (The co-op flat. Interior 1926). The photo and the interior have meanwhile become modernist icons and Hannes Meyer's trademarks. Hannes Meyer first published the photo in 1926 in his equally well-known manifesto, DIE NEUE WELT (The new world)

"The only project that makes logical use of the high-rise as an operational instrument for the General Secretariat is the (successful) project by the Swiss architects Wittwer and Meyer. Alongside Corbusier's, it should shortly become one of the best known in the competition, for it contains the most innovative elements that are open to development."

Sigfried Giedion, "Architecture at the turning point" from:
"Neue Zürcher Zeitung", Sunday, 24.7.1927, p. 4

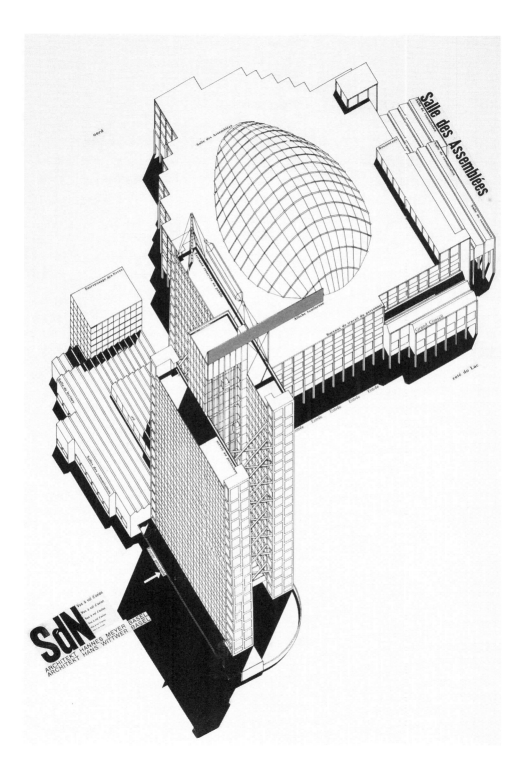

nord

Salle des Assemblées

Salle des Assemblées

Restaurant

Entrepôsage des livres

Affiche lumineuse

Bureaux de travail du personnel

Grand Conseil

côté du Lac

Entrée Entrée Entrée Entrée

SdN

ARCHITEKT HANNES MEYER BASEL
ARCHITEKT HANS WITTWER BASEL

Hannes Meyer and Hans Wittwer, design for the
Petersschule building in Basel, 1927, revised version
of the design submitted for the 1926 competition

ABC – Hannes Meyer and the Avant-garde

In 1923 Hannes Meyer was embroiled in an existential professional crisis. He was no longer able to reconcile his neoclassi-
cal design approach with his own concept of a collective society. For a time, he withdrew completely from the practice of
architecture. In 1924 the recently formed avant-garde group
ABC based around Emil Roth, Hans Schmidt and Mart Stam in
collaboration with El Lissitzky provided the impetus needed to
put the crisis behind him. Their radical pursuit of new, elemen-
tary forms of expression beyond what they perceived as out-
dated, individualistic concepts of art inspired Meyer to critical
design studies in the sphere of constructivist art. In 1926 he
was given the opportunity to publish his artistic research in a
special edition of the ABC group's journal. In the same year he
made his return as an architect with his design for the Petersschule building in Basel.

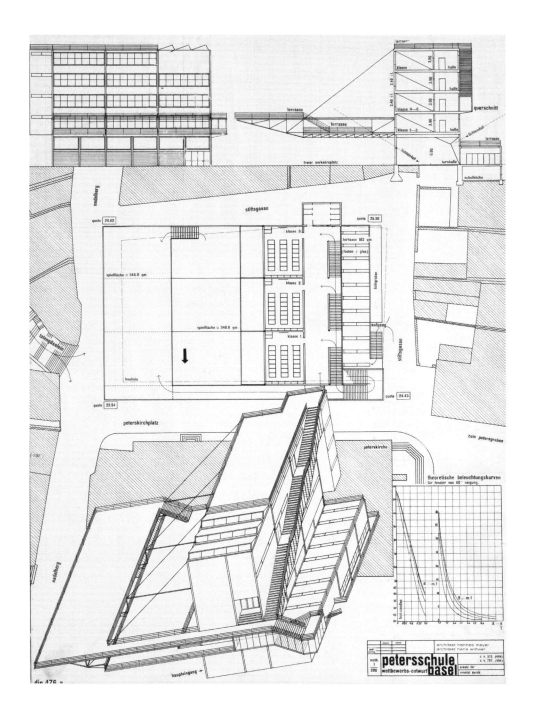

terrasse

klasse · halle · 3.90

klasse · halle · 3.90

klasse 4—6 · halle · 3.90

querschnitt

terrasse

klasse 1—3 · halle · 6.00

lichtentfall

terrasse

turnhalle

schulküche

freier verkehrsplatz

nadelberg

stiftsgasse

quote 24.62

quote 25.20

klasse 3.

terrasse 162 qm
(beton + glas)

spielfläche = 345.0 qm

lichtgraben

klasse 2

spielfläche = 340.0 qm

aufgang

klasse 1.

stiftsgasse

baulinie

quote 23.94

quote 24.43

totengässlein

peterskirchplatz

peterskirche

zum petersgraben

nadelberg

theoretische beleuchtungskurven
für fenster von 60° neigung

haupteingang

din 476.2

architekt hannes meyer
architekt hans wittwer

d. k. 372. (404)
d. k. 727. (494)

ersatz für
ersetzt durch

peterschule
basel

wettbewerbs-entwurf

1
200

Education

When Gropius appointed Hannes Meyer at the Bauhaus in 1927, the latter had no teaching experience whatsoever. In terms of content, Meyer continued on the path that he had taken in previous years among the Swiss avant-garde. In classes, his methodology pursued the aim of interdisciplinary teamwork in so-called vertical brigades, thereby favouring work on real, rather than hypothetical, projects.

With his appointment as director of the Bauhaus in 1928, Hannes Meyer continued to push this development. He implemented substantial educational reforms at the school, closing the distance between the opposite poles of science and art and emphasising the social content of projects. "Volksbedarf statt Luxusbedarf" (The needs of the people instead of the need for luxury) became the new motto. Meyer's thinking thereby became increasingly radical, taking him from the cooperative collective to Marxism, whereupon he was dismissed without notice from the Bauhaus in summer 1930.

During his subsequent tenure at the WASI Institute, Moscow in Stalinist Russia, Meyer unsuccessfully called for the absorption of education in urban development and architecture in the apparatus of the state in symbiosis with politics and economy in a new collective society. In the ensuing period in Mexico, after two years Meyer also floundered at the newly founded institute for urban development and planning.

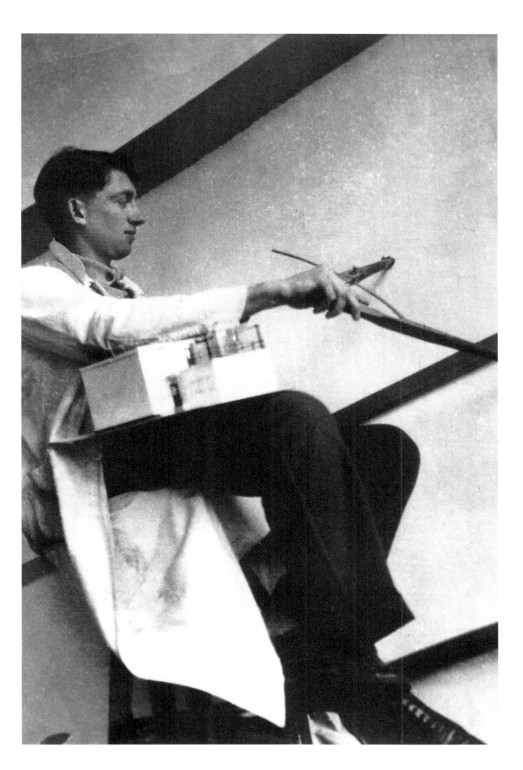

Diagram from Paul Klee's diary showing the organisational structure of the Bauhaus Dessau under the leadership of Hannes Meyer, 1928

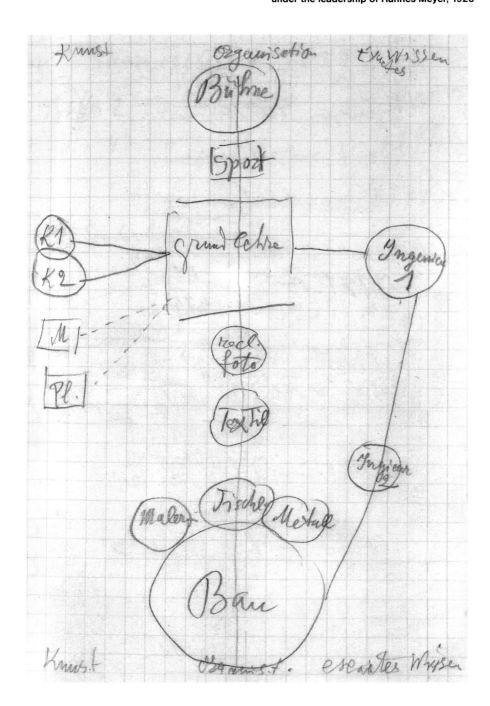

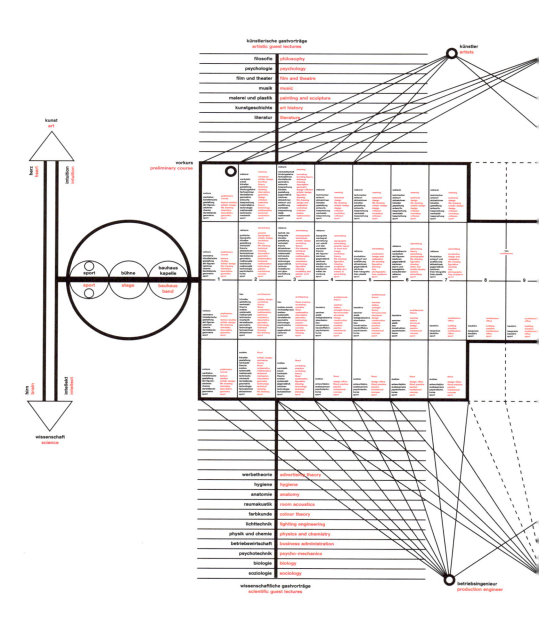

Organisational structure of the Bauhaus Dessau, 1930, new drawing by the Hochschule für Architektur und Bauwesen Weimar (HAB), ca. 1987, and Prill Vieceli Cremers, 2015

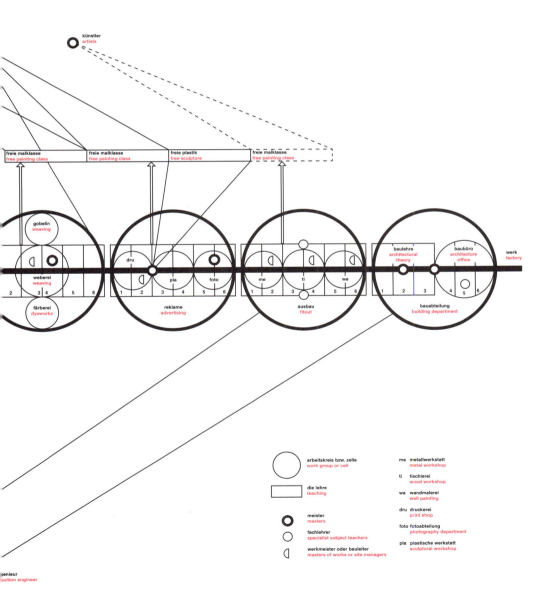

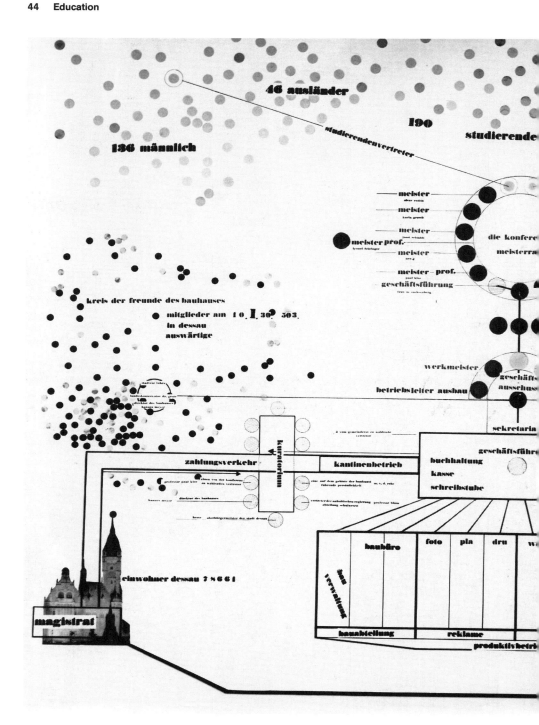

46 ausländer

190

studierende

136 männlich

studierendenvertreter

meister
meister
meister
meister prof.
meister
meister – prof.
geschäftsführung

die konfere
meisterra

kreis der freunde des bauhauses

mitglieder am 1 0. I 30² 503
in dessau
auswärtige

werkmeister
geschäfts
ausschuss

betriebsleiter ausbau

sekretaria

geschäftsführ
buchhaltung
kasse
schreibstube

zahlungsverkehr

kuratorium

kantinenbetrieb

baubüro   foto   pla   dru   w

hau
verwaltung

einwohner dessau 7 × 6 6 1

magistrat

hauabteilung   reklame

produktivbetr

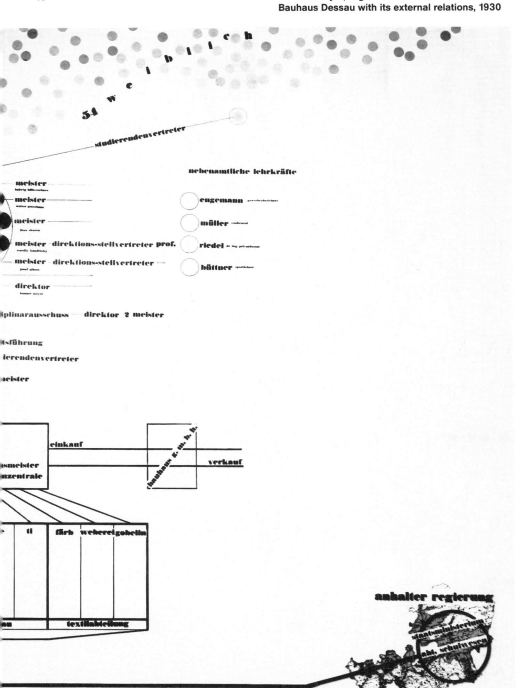

z w e i b l i c h

54

studierendenvertreter

meister
ludwig hilberseimer

meister
walter peterhans

meister
lina chase

meister direktions-stellvertreter prof.
vassily kandinsky

meister direktions-stellvertreter
josef albers

direktor
hannes meyer

nebenamtliche lehrkräfte

engemann gewerbeoberlehrer

müller studienrat

riedel dr. ing. privatdozent

büttner sportlehrer

plinarausschuss — direktor 2 meister

sführung

ierendenvertreter

eister

einkauf

smeister
nzentrale

bauhaus G. m. b. h.

verkauf

d färb weberei gobelin

au textilabteilung

anhalter regierung

staatsministerium

abt. schulwesen

Students Ali Sefi Halil Bey, Hubert Hoffmann, Arieh
Sharon and unknown (from top to bottom) at the
Bauhaus Dessau, ca. 1929

Students in the Bauhaus Dessau's building department working on the competition for the
Berlin-Haselhorst housing estate, 1929

Students Albert Mentzel, Georg Hartmann (with
epee), Myriam Manuckiam and Naftalie Rubinstein
on the sports field of the Bauhaus building in
Dessau, 1928, photo: T. Lux Feininger

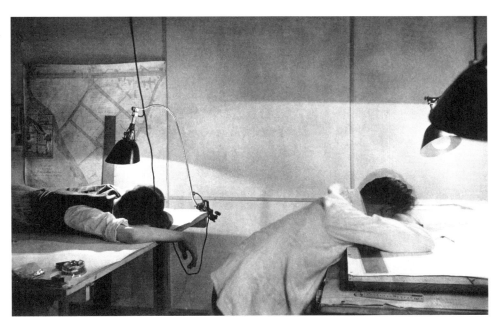

Hannes Meyer attending a lecture at the University
of Architecture (W.A.S.I.) in Moscow, late 1930,
documentation by the former Bauhaus student
Konrad Püschel

"160 Millionen der Sowjetunion laden deutsche Arbeiter ein."
Hannes Meyer spricht vor Studenten und Lehrkräften der Moskauer Archi-
tektur-Hochschule - WASI - 1930

In 1939 Hannes Meyer responded to the call of the President of
Mexico, Lázaro Cárdenas del Río, for the foundation of an
Institute for Urban Development and Planning at the National
Polytechnic Institute (IPN) in Mexico City. From the outset,
Meyer was at loggerheads with Guillermo Terrés, director of
the University of Engineering and Architecture and head of the
school administration at IPN. In 1941 at Terrés' request Meyer,
in collaboration with José Luis Cuevas and Enrique Yáñez,
drew up a revised organisation and lesson plan with the disci-
plines Theory, History, Economics, Communication, Region
and Landscape, Weather, Hygiene, Housing and Law. The very
same year, Meyer's institute was closed due to lack of funding.

Hannes Meyer, alternative version of an organisational structure for the Institute for Urban Development and Planning at the National Polytechnic Institute (IPN) in Mexico City, 1941

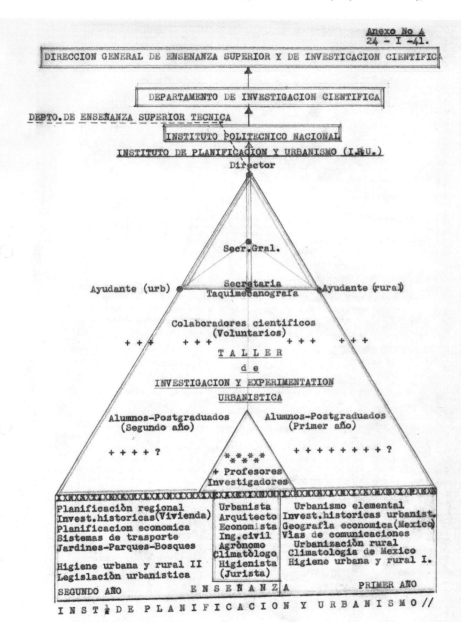

Politics and Migration

"young people! what do you seek in the art academies? come to the bauhaus!" was the upbeat appeal issued by the new Bauhaus director Hannes Meyer in 1928. But even the resignation of his predecessor Walter Gropius had been impelled by a series of fundamental problems in the Bauhaus and the city of Dessau. The resulting conflicts intensified in the era of Hannes Meyer and led in August 1930 to his politically motivated dismissal. The controversies and crises not only reflected the politically and socially dysfunctional climate of the Weimar Republic, but also affected the everyday lives and perspectives of the directors, teaching staff and students at the Bauhaus. Parts of the student body became politically radicalised, splitting the Bauhaus into a communist and a moderate faction. In order to keep the Bauhaus going amidst this confusion, in 1930 leading politicians of the centre and centre-left appointed Ludwig Mies van der Rohe as the new director. The successes of the National Socialists in both municipal and federal state elections heralded the end for the Bauhaus, in 1932 in Dessau and 1933 in Berlin.

Communist students at the Bauhaus with the third issue of their magazine "bauhaus. organ des kostufra" with articles about Hannes Meyer's dismissal without notice, 1930

Bauhaus students protest against Hannes Meyer's dismissal, Dessau, 1930

Studio building of the Bauhaus Dessau with Nazi flag, 1932

Architecture

Hannes Meyer radically overturned the concept of the architect as an omnipotent master builder. In his practice of architecture, his systematic progression from independent to Marxist architect occurred over the course of his office partnership with Hans Wittwer. In his view, the architect, like every other designer, intellectual and worker, was no more and no less than a serving member of society. As in his teaching method with the vertical brigades, Meyer advocated the principle of collaborative work in architecture and planning. "I never develop projects alone" was his credo. Significant examples include the plans for the expansion of the Dessau-Törten housing estate, the construction of the school of the ADGB (Federation of German Trade Unions) in Bernau by Berlin and the unrealised housing estate for workers, Lomas de Becerra, in Mexico.

The composition of the team relied on the idea that the more varied the competencies of the collaborators, the more effective and creative the results. The building programmes were to evolve from scientifically founded analytical processes. Fact-finding processes were consistently informed by technical-industrial, political-economical and psychological-artistic factors. Accordingly, Meyer advocated a scientifically rationalised and standardized methodology for graphic representation based on the DIN-Code of the German Institute for Standardization or the Soviet Gosudarstwenny Standard (GOST).

philipp tolziner

Neubau der Laubenganghäuser in Dessau-Törten
im Jahre 1929

Documentation of the construction process of the
balcony access houses in Dessau-Törten in 1929
by the Bauhaus student Konrad Püschel, n.y.

Neubau der Laubenganghäuser in Dessau-Törten
im Jahre 1929

Building department of the Bauhaus Dessau, plans
for the expansion of the Dessau-Törten housing
estate, 1930

Building department of the Bauhaus Dessau, floor
plans, elevations, cross sections and statistical
data pertaining to the balcony access houses for
the Dessau-Törten housing estate, 1930

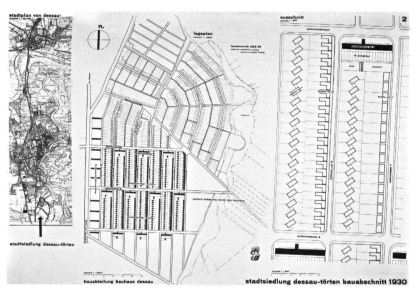

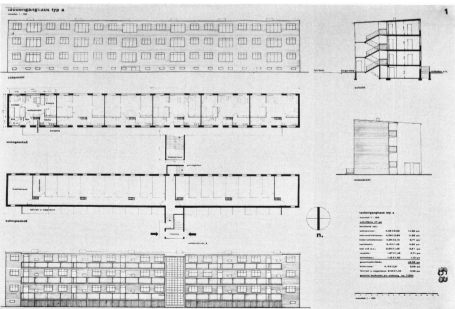

Balcony access houses after completion with residents, photographer unknown

South and north view of one of the balcony access houses on the Dessau-Törten housing estate, 1930, photographer unknown

Maurerbrigadier   Bauarbeiter Konrad Püschel
        Zimmerer Brigadier
              Praktikant
                 Ludwig

Püschel
   Ludwig

Neubau der ADGB-Schule in Berlin
Baubudenscenen

Documentation of the construction process, topping-out ceremony and opening of the school of the ADGB (Federation of German Trade Unions) in Bernau by Berlin in 1929-1930 by the Bauhaus students and apprentices on the building site, Konrad Püschel, n.y.

Neubau der Schule des ADGB in Bernau bei Berlin
Haupteingang.

Lehrerwohnungen

Neubau der Schule des ADGB in Bernau bei Berlin
Sharon als Bauleiter der Lehrerhäuser

Neubau der Schule des ADGB in Bernau bei Berlin
Der Baustellenhund

Bauarbeiter - Praktikant
Konrad Püschel hat die
Richtkrone hochgezogen.
Polier Krüger hält den
Richtspruch.

Neben Fahrrad
Fritz Luhr

mit Spazierstock
daipart.Vorsitzen.
der des ADGB

Neubau der Schule des ADGB in Bernau bei Berlin
Richtfest

Hannes Meyer and Hans Wittwer with the
assistance of the Bauhaus Dessau, main entrance
of the completed school of the ADGB (Federation
of German Trade Unions) in Bernau by Berlin,
1930, photo: Walter Peterhans

The three high chimneys next to the entrance were not part of the competition entry submitted by Hannes Meyer and Hans Wittwer. They were first added in the implementation planning, probably at the request of the ADGB, and were designed to symbolise the three pillars of the Federation, i.e., workers, employees and civil servants – a symbolism that went against Hannes Meyer's universal and collective design practice.

View from the library to the halls of residence, 1930, photo: Walter Peterhans

Basin to wash feet in the glazed area before the entrance to the sports hall, 1930, photo: Walter Peterhans

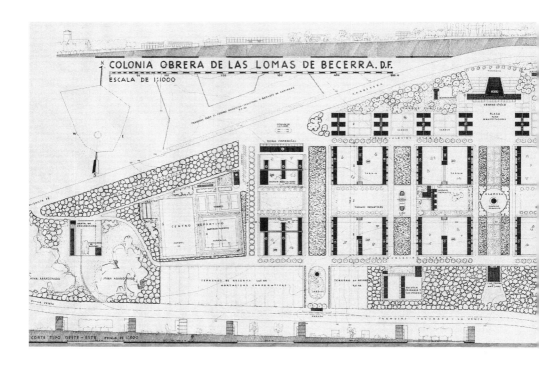

Raúl Cacho, Hannes Meyer, Humberto Cos and
Kay B. Adams, design for the workers' housing
estate Lomas de Becerra near the industrial zone
Tacubaya, San Pedro de los Pinos, Mexico,
1942/43

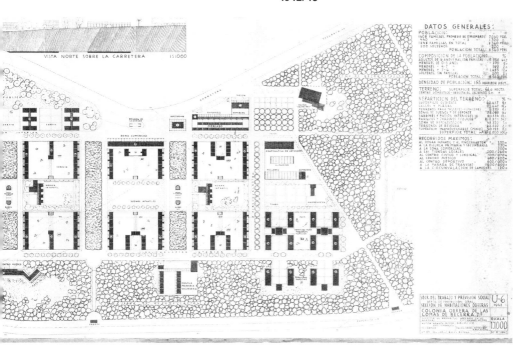

The plans identify Raúl Cacho as project leader, Hannes
Meyer as adviser and Hannes Meyer, Kay B. Adams and
Humberto Cos as a collective development team.

Migration and Politics

Hannes Meyer's reputation at the Bauhaus and his migrations to post-revolutionary Russia and Mexico were completely consistent with his conceptual ideas geared to shaping a new, collective society. They were never pathways to exile. As a Swiss citizen, this problem did not occur to him. That all these paths ultimately ended in failure was due to the respective political circumstances and Meyer's errors of judgement. Following his dismissal from the Bauhaus Dessau in 1930 and his subsequent sojourn in the Soviet Union, Meyer left the latter in 1936, just before the onset of ethnic cleansing. A planned fresh start in Spain was stymied by the victory of the Franco regime. The optimistic beginning in Mexico in 1939 also came to a sudden end the following year after a change of government. In addition to unsuccessful planning commissions, Meyer was thereafter primarily involved in upholding the collective ideals of the Mexican revolution through his collaboration in the socialist artists' group Taller de Gráfica Popular (TGP) and in the activities of European exiles in Mexico protesting against the terrors of the Nazi regime in Europe. In late 1949 Meyer finally returned to his home in Switzerland.

Graphics for the first pages of El Libro Negro
(The black book) on the Nazi terror in Europe

Title page of El Libro Negro (The black book) on
the Nazi terror in Europe, edited by Antonio Castro
Leal, André Simone, Bodo Uhse, Juan Rejano,
Anna Seghers, Ludwig Renn and Egon Erwin
Kisch, picture editor, Hannes Meyer, Mexico,
1.2.1943

A page from "Album TGP México" with drawings
by Hannes Meyer and his wife Lena Bergner. The
album was published in 1949 by the artists' group
Taller de Gráfica Popular (TGP) as a record of
12 years of collective collaboration. The picture
editor was Hannes Meyer.

A todos los que murieron
A todos los que están luchando

LENA BERGNER: El Ajusco, visto desde el Valle de Contreras, D. F.
Grabado, 27,5 × 20,5 cm. 1947.
The Ajusco mountain, seen from the Valley of Contreras, D. F.

HANNES MEYER: Amate-tree.
Dibujo, 35 × 29 cm. 1948.

136
Artistas - Huéspedes

Landscape

The connection to the landscape in Hannes Meyer's work best reveals the emotional qualities and lines of development in his creative oeuvre. Here, alongside the purely functional approaches of Marxist economics and politics, he deployed his third mainstay in architecture and planning: the psychological-artistic element. On the one hand, we have the scientific mastery of natural influences on human existence and ways of living, such as climate, the position of the sun, and geology; on the other, the highly individual characterisations of landscape as the expression of homeland, of "home", of regionally specific architecture as identification of place. This process is exemplified by the school of the ADGB (Federation of German Trade Unions) in Bernau by Berlin, the children's home in Mümliswil, the Jewish enclave Birobidzhan in Russia and the spa of Agua Hedionda in Mexico.

In 1929 he articulated this approach succinctly at the end of his lyrical text bauhaus und gesellschaft (bauhaus and society): "a conscious experience of the landscape is building as determined by fate. as creators we fulfil the fate of the landscape." This deep-seated commitment to landscape likewise marked a departure from the previously propagandised global design "Esperanto" manifested in Hannes Meyer's 1926 plans for the League of Nations building in Geneva.

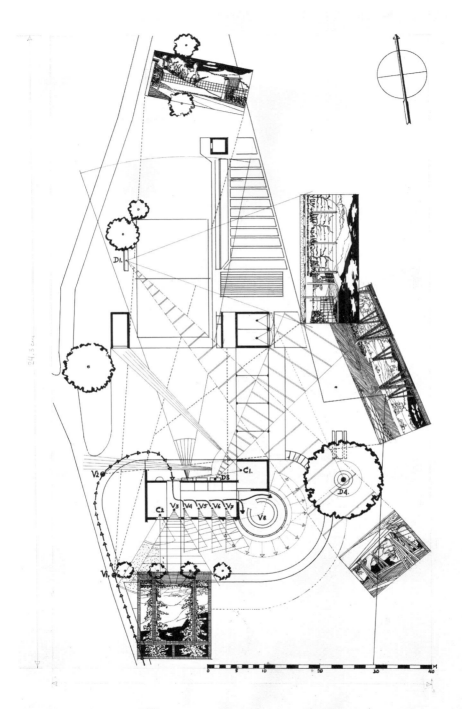

View of the landscape from the roof terrace, over the round room and along the employee block, 1939

View of the landscape from the roof terrace, over the round room along the children's wing, 1939

Co-operative children's home in Mümliswil, view of the landscape over the employee block and the round room, 1939

73

Hannes Meyer explains his design for the
co-operative children's home in Mümliswil to,
among others, Bernhard Jäggi, a native of
Mümliswil, initiator of the housing co-operative
Freidorf and president of the directorate of the
association of Swiss consumer societies, 1937/38,
photographer unknown

Furnishing in the round room, 1939

View of the children's home from the southeast,
1939

Hannes Meyer, page 1 of the site plans for the
administrative centre of the Jewish Autonomous
Oblast Birobidzhan in Siberia, 1933/34

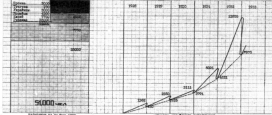

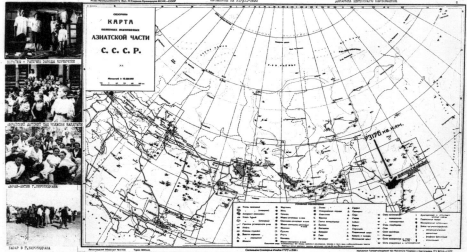

Views and documentation of the landscape and
everyday life in Birobidzhan for the development
plans, 1933, photo: Hannes Meyer

Hannes Meyer in Birobidzhan, 1933, photographer
unknown

Hannes Meyer, town planning and landscape
studies and plans for the spa of Agua Hedionda in
Mexico, 1947

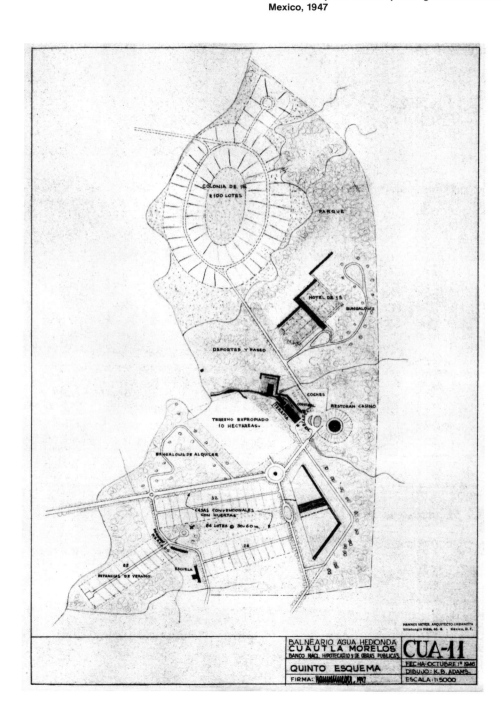

Chart of the monthly temperature fluctuations in Aguda Hedionda, 1946

Evaluation and comparison of the composition of the water in Agua Hedionda based on chemical, bacteriological and radioactive analyses, 1946

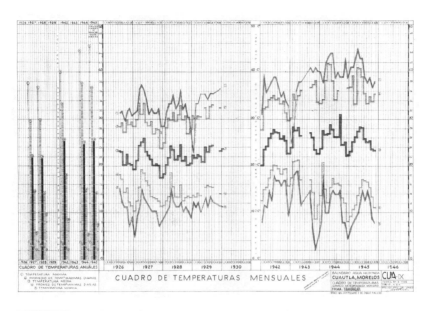

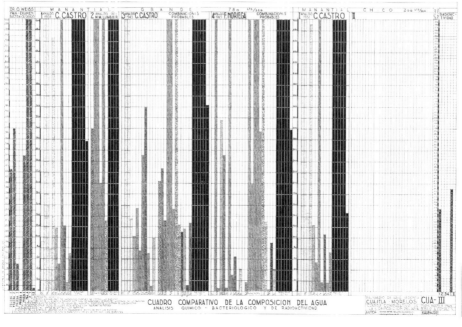

Reception and Marginalisation

While an objective reception of Hannes Meyer's character and work took until the late 1980, this cannot be ascribed solely to his membership of the extreme left spectrum of modernism. This process of marginalisation began as early as 1928 with his appointment as director of the Bauhaus. Meyer failed to align the Bauhaus internally to his socialist goals while simultaneously presenting it as neutral to the outside world, to successfully steer its course through the politically sensitive times.

The well-founded anxiety about the existence of the Bauhaus led to a permanent break with his supporters, most notably Walter Gropius. Bauhaus was already a brand name. Meyer's dismissal without notice inevitably became a full-blown scandal, from which he was never to recover.

The wealth of articles and activities relating to Hannes Meyer's work mean that one can no longer speak of a lack of acknowledgement. Whether his work will ever become as popular as that of the other two Bauhaus directors, Walter Gropius and Mies van der Rohe, is a separate issue.

You will find a comprehensive bibliography of Hannes Meyer
on the homepage www.bauhaus-dessau.de, under the heading Library.

Paul Camenisch, portrait of
Hannes Meyer, 1952/53

"hannes was always the inferiority complex-type among the communists, that's why he betrayed them to the right and sweet-talked them to the left. mies did things that protected them much more than the things hannes did. [...] under hannes, everything was hysterical. but! mies as spiritual guide is of course nothing. spiritually, everything happens in opposition to the leader"

Georg Schmidt about his time at the Bauhaus Dessau in 1931, from a letter to Hans Schmidt, Binningen, 11.1.1932. Georg Schmidt was a committed socialist and a younger brother of Hans Schmidt, co-founder of the Swiss avant-garde group ABC.

Ernst Kállai, caricature of Hannes Meyer, "Co-op der Bauhausverkehrssittenschutzengel" (Co-op of the Bauhausacceptedstandardsguardianangel), 1930

Hannes Meyer's Network – Continuity and Breaks

Astrid Volpert for the
DFG Bauhaus Project "Bewegte Netze"

Meyer lived without Wi-Fi and Smartphone. In his day, telephone calls had a limited range. For these reasons alone, it is remarkable how well informed he always was about people outside his personal circle, about Europe and global events and their repercussions. Meyer moved restlessly from one place to the next. Over long distances, he counted the rail joints he passed over on his train journeys, or travelled by ship from country to country. On foot, he went on expeditions into remote regions far removed from urban milieus. In the far east of the Soviet Union, as in Mexico's high valleys, he conducted research into nature and ethnography.

The experiences he gathered on several continents formed the basis for his objectives and projects, one of which was his network. This forged Meyer's worldview, his approach to the challenges of the time. As an architect, a citizen and later, a comrade, he wanted to be the designer of the "new world". His dense network of relationships with people of different generations and backgrounds – one that responded flexibly to changes – lasted for four decades. This most important medium of exchange from 1930 evolved into a databank of vital contacts and correspondence.

The passion and care with which the architect and urbanist built up and cultivated his network under challenging circumstances (frequent change of address, isolation of exile) is shown by the extensive holdings of the architect's estate at the Deutsches Architekturmuseum (DAM) in Frankfurt. This includes post from or to more than 120 contact persons and

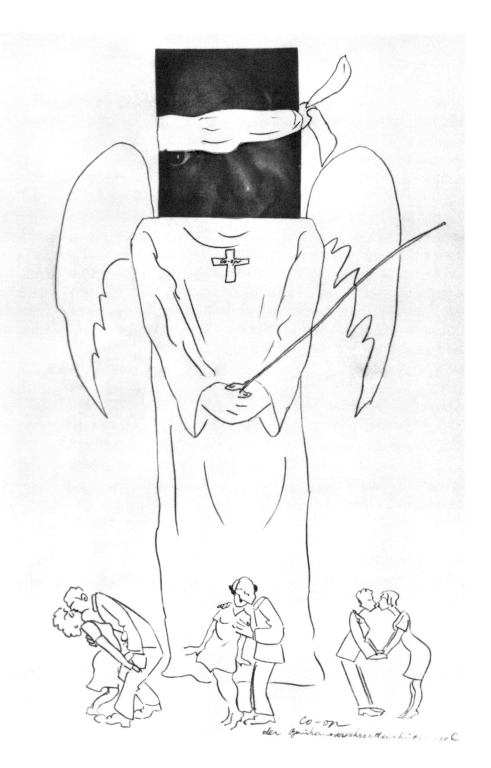

co-on
der Bauhausverschvelten Schutzengel

institutions with whom Meyer communicated from the mid-1920s until a year before his death. Predominantly, these are professional associates – architects, painters, sculptors, illustrators, and also activists of every political colour and nationality from Italy, the USSR, the USA and Mexico. Meyer communicated in five foreign languages. Despite the meticulous preservation of originals and copies, there are nevertheless significant gaps. Those who wish to gain a precise picture of Meyer's activity in Moscow must also look for archives elsewhere. After 1951 Meyer admitted to a Swiss architect that he had "cremated" many letters. He wanted to be preserved for posterity as a successful man who fought a consistent battle. He set himself apart from doubt, conflicts and defeats.

What makes reading the letters of the radical left-wing proponent of modernism so fascinating and gripping today, beyond news of his innovations in design, is the evidence of the social, economic and political changes in his life. Who was on his side and who disagreed with him, who was allowed to stay in the network and who he left behind is explained in around 50 biographies about philosophers, economists, teachers, artists, architects and politicians. The network's connections range from early twentieth century Swiss and German social reformers to members of the European art avant-gardes, through to Mexican folk artists.

Following his politically motivated dismissal as director of the Bauhaus, and as a failed functionalist architect and professor in Moscow, Meyer radicalised his political stance. He broke with the Marxism of Western intellectuals and became a committed Stalinist. This transition marks the break with former friends, among them many Bauhauslers who had gone with him to the USSR. Cut off from direct contacts to

Europe during WWII, after 1945 Meyer reactivated and up-dated his network anew from Mexico. He excluded collabo-rators with the Nazi regime, but also alleged spies convicted in the Stalinist repressions. Back in Europe, a lack of income and increasingly poor health limited his mobility. At the time of Stalin's death in March 1953, Hannes Meyer lived in Ticino. He fell forever silent in 1954.

**Hannes Meyer
(18 November 1889, Basel – 19 July 1954, Crocifisso di
Savosa) – architect, urbanist**

**1905–1909
Apprenticeship as a mason, training as an architectural
draughtsman and foreman, attendance at the vocational
school in Basel**

**1909–1912
Work in the offices of Albert Fröhlich and Emil Schaudt in
Berlin, evening courses at the school of arts and crafts,
academy of agriculture and the town planning institute of TH
Berlin**

**1912/13
Study trip to England**

**1916–1918
Assistant to Georg Metzendorf in Munich, then architect at
the Krupp building headquarters in Essen**

**1919–1921
Design and construction of the co-operative housing estate
Freidorf in Muttenz, Switzerland**

**1923–1926
Prototypes of new design and art, "Theatre Co-op" in Ghent,
Belgium**

**1926/27
With Hans Wittwer, competition entries for the Petersschule
building in Basel and the General Secretariat of the League
of Nations in Geneva**

1927–1930
**Master of Architecture at the Bauhaus Dessau, from April
1928 Director of the Bauhaus Dessau, dismissed without
notice on 1 August 1930**

1928–1930
**With Hans Wittwer, students and the Bauhaus workshops,
design and construction of the school of the ADGB (Federation of German Trade Unions) in Bernau by Berlin and 90
'Volkswohnungen' (People's flats) in Dessau-Törten**

1930–1936
**Town planner and propagandist in the USSR, chief architect
in three building trusts (plans for new industrial towns for
8,000–250,000 inhabitants), professor at the Moscow Architectural Institute (1930–1933), research professor at the
Academy of Architecture (1934/35)**

1936–1939
Architect in Geneva, children's home in Mümliswil

1939–1949
**Chief architect and pedagogue in Mexico city, inter alia at
the national institute for town planning and in the national
committee for school building; with Lena Meyer-Bergner,
edition of prints for Taller de Gráfica Popular (workshop
cooperative for graphic folk art)**

1949–1954
Work in Ticino on albums about the Bauhaus

Explanatory text from the presentation of the
Volkswohnung (People's flat) of the Bauhaus
Dessau in Grassi Museum Leipzig, 1929

New prototypes from the 'Volkswohnung'

Werner Möller
Research Associate
Bauhaus Dessau Foundation

The 'Volkswohnung' (People's flat) by Hannes Meyer was a statement about the reorientation of the Bauhaus under his leadership. While the designs for interiors in the era of his predecessor Walter Gropius mainly catered to the discerning demands of a new middle class of white-collar workers and modern-minded intellectuals, the 'Volkswohnung' adopted a position that firmly countered this trend. Its products were not designed to be decorative, but implicitly practical, durable and affordable for all.

One indication of this in the production of furniture was the rejection of the tubular steel that is now so characteristic of the Bauhaus. Under Meyer, the use of this material was limited to just a few designs. In the times of crisis, tubular steel furniture was simply too expensive for the ordinary worker. The solution was wood and the minimisation of material consumption, pushed to the extreme structural limits. In order to be serviceable for subsistence-level housing, aspects such as the furniture's lightness, versatility and facility for assembly/disassembly were likewise important. The display of the 1929 'Volkswohnung' exhibition in the Grassi Museum Leipzig provided a perfect example.

But unlike the Bauhaus wallpapers, textiles and lamps of the 'Volkswohnung', the furniture proved to be a failure. Neither industry nor public were ever interested in these products. Only a few buildings were furnished with these pieces, such as the school of the ADGB (Federation of German Trade

kein schmuckes heim, glück allein

sondern eine brauchbare volkswohnung zu zeigen, ist sinn und zweck der bauhaus-räume im grassi-museum.

eine brauchbare volkswohnung muß billig sein. die bauhaus-wohnung ist billig durch äußerste platzausnutzung, minimale raummasse, zeitsparende prakt. einrichtung.

zwei räume, zugleich wohn- und schlafzimmer. klappbare betten, bei tage hochgeklappt — des nachts heruntergeklappt. sich gleichbleibende schrankeinheiten; versetzbare zwischenböden ermöglichen verschiedene raumeinteilung, somit verschiedene verwendung. minimale tiefe der schränke, günstiges kleiderhängen durch herausschwenkbare kleiderhaken.

küche: maßgebend war die forderung, der hausfrau jede überflüssige bewegung zu ersparen.

der waschraum: mit waschbecken und handbrause hat im bau einen vertieften wasserabführenden boden.

wände mit bauhaustapeten: keine ornamente, sondern kleinste musterung als struktur wirkend. daher restlose ausnutzung der tapetenräume ohne jeden abfall.

beleuchtung: gleichmäßig verteiltes einwandfreies licht durch kandem-lampen (bauhaus-modell). verwendet wurden ueue errungenschaften der haushaltstechnik, um der frau das arbeiten im hause möglichst zu erleichtern.

die demonstrationstafeln zeigen, wie die bauhausarbeit auf den verbrauch gerichtet ist. das schmückende vermeiden, das praktische fördern. nicht der luxus, einerlei ob handwerklicher oder maschinentechnischer art, sondern das bedürfnis der breitesten volksgemeinschaft ist maßgebend.

tafel 1   zerlegbarer sessel von josef albers. davor der fertige sessel.

tafel 2   entwicklung der beleuchtung von der kerze bis zur neuen bauhaustischlampe.

tafel 3   neue versuche der bauhaus-weberei. abwaschbare und schalldämpfende wandstoffe. proben aus dem musterbuche.

tafel 4   neue arbeit der metallwerkstatt: küchenhocker aus stahlrohr, einfachste konstruktion. vor der tafel fertiges mod.

tafel 5   abgenutzter kinderstuhl zur demonstration, daß eine schleiflack-lackierung für solche möbel unangebracht ist. dagegen: beispiele verschiedener holzbehandlungen, die für möbel am besten geeignet sind. — versuchsergebnisse die das verhalten verschiedener lacke gegen feuer und säure veranschaulichen.

die „volkswohnung"
ausgestellt vom bauhaus dessau

Unions) in Bernau by Berlin. At the same time, both conceptually and design-wise, in their rigorous purist aesthetic and pursuit of perfection these pieces were by no means inferior to the early tubular steel furniture designed by Marcel Breuer. However, their target group was decidedly different: the working class. These designs show no signs of the inherent crudeness in materiality or execution, the manifestations of a shortage of resources, or of the DIY approach of the contemporary furniture of the company Hartz IV-Möbel.

The increasing pressure to economise at the Bauhaus in the late-1920s was also expressed in the way the furniture was marketed. Instead of being listed in an elaborately designed and printed "Catalogue of samples" as they were under Walter Gropius, each model was promoted using small fact sheets and simple blueprints in A5 format.

For the exhibition "The Co-op Principle – Hannes Meyer and the Concept of Collective Design" two prototypes of furniture from the 'Volkswohnung' were remade based on these templates in cooperation with the apprentices' workshop of the Deutsche Werkstätten Hellerau (DWH). These are the simplest furniture designs in the entire 'Volkswohnung' product range: the stool ti 245 and the table ti 207. The design of the stool is ascribed to the Bauhaus student Howard Dearstyne; the designer of the table is unknown. The construction principle for both pieces probably dates back to Josef Albers.

In some aspects of their execution, the new prototypes from the DWH deviate from the models produced at the Bauhaus. However, the historic versions of the furniture for the 'Volkswohnung' also departed from the self-imposed worthy aims of the Bauhaus in a few decisive ways, for

The new prototypes of stool ti 245 and table ti 207 made in the apprentices' workshop of the Deutsche Werkstätten Hellerau, 2015, photo: Tobias Kandt

Fragmented framework of table ti 207, from: "bauhaus. vierteljahr-zeitschrift für gestaltung" 3 (1929) 2, p. 23, photographer unknown

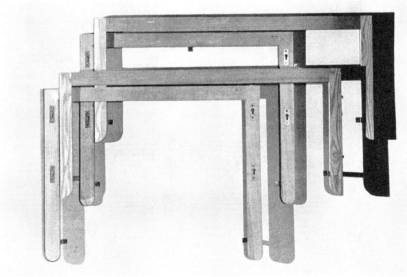

bauhaus dessau tischlerei
ti 245

hocker
sitzhöhe
45 cm

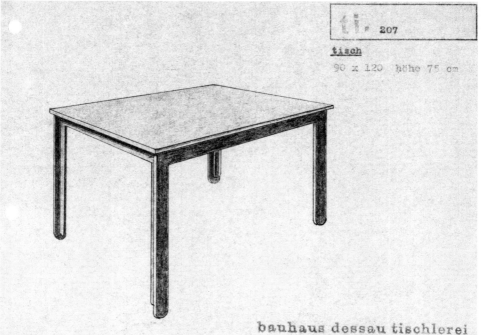

ti 207

tisch
90 x 120   höhe 75 cm

bauhaus dessau tischlerei

purely pragmatic reasons: Instead of the new nitrocellu-
lose paints advertised in the fact sheets, which proved
problematic in practice, all furniture orders at the Bauhaus
were treated with the traditional shellac; the furniture was
also evidently made from readily available types of wood,
such as ash or sycamore, rather than beech or oak. For the
finish of the new prototypes, the fact sheets therefore
provided orientation for the choice of wood, and oak was
selected. The currently widely used hard wax oil was cho-
sen to treat the surfaces. A comparable substitute had to
be found for the material used to cover the stools, because
iron or horsehair yarns matching the originals are not
commercially available today. Based on the new prototypes, a small series of six stools and tables in copper
beech were produced for the exhibition by the Arbeits- und
Sozialförderungsgesellschaft Dessau e.V. (ASG).

p. 66 / 67
Bauhaus Dessau Foundation (Estate Hannes Meyer)

p. 69
gta Archiv / ETH Zürich
gta Archiv / ETH Zürich
gta Archiv / ETH Zürich

p. 71
gta Archiv / ETH Zürich

p. 72 / 73
Deutsches Architekturmuseum, Frankfurt am Main
Deutsches Architekturmuseum, Frankfurt am Main
gta Archiv / ETH Zürich
Bauhaus Dessau Foundation (Estate Hannes Meyer)
Deutsches Architekturmuseum, Frankfurt am Main
Deutsches Architekturmuseum, Frankfurt am Main

p. 74 / 75
Deutsches Architekturmuseum, Frankfurt am Main
Bauhaus Dessau Foundation (Estate Hannes Meyer)
Bauhaus Dessau Foundation (Estate Hannes Meyer)

p. 76 / 77
Bauhaus Dessau Foundation (Estate Hannes Meyer)
Bauhaus Dessau Foundation (Estate Hannes Meyer)
Bauhaus Dessau Foundation (Estate Hannes Meyer)

p. 79
Kunstmuseum Olten (Deposit of Freunde
Kunstmuseum Olten 2006)

p. 81
Bauhaus-Archiv Berlin

p. 87
Bauhaus Dessau Foundation

p. 89
Bauhaus Dessau Foundation
Bauhaus Dessau Foundation

p. 90
Bauhaus Dessau Foundation

The Bauhaus Dessau Foundation owns the usage
rights of the work of Hannes Meyer, which were
tranferred by Ms. Livia Meyer-Klee.

The Co-op Principle – Hannes Meyer and the Concept of Collective Design

in the Bauhaus Dessau
from 21 May to 4 October 2015

in the Architekturmuseum München
(Pinakothek der Moderne)
from 17 March to 12 June 2016

Catalogue

Publisher
Werner Möller in collaboration with Raquel Franklin for the Bauhaus Dessau Foundation

Editors
Werner Möller, Tim Leik

Copy editors
Karola Handwerker Heinze,
Katrin Globke, Benita Weise

Translations
Rebecca Philipps Williams,
Katrin Globke

Design
Prill Vieceli Cremers
In collaboration with Emanuel Heim

Printers
PögeDruck, Leipzig

Published by

Spector Books
Harkortstraße 10
04107 Leipzig, Germany
www.spectorbooks.com

Germany, Austria: GVA, Gemeinsame Verlagsauslieferung Göttingen GmbH&Co. KG
www.gva-verlage.de
Switzerland: AVA Verlagsauslieferung AG,
www.ava.ch

The German edition of the book also published
under following ISBN 978-3-95905-009-8 by
Spector Books.

Printed in Germany

First edition

ISBN 978-3-95905-010-4

Cover photo:
Hannes Meyer surveying the building site of the
school of the Federation of German Trade Unions
in Bernau by Berlin, 1928, photo: Erich Consemüller, Bauhaus Dessau Foundation,
© Stephan Consemüller

Edition Bauhaus 48

Bauhaus Dessau Foundation
Gropiusallee 38
06846 Dessau-Roßlau, Germany
www.bauhaus-dessau.de

Christo
Jeanne-Claude

Collective 37

95

Exhibition

Curators
Raquel Franklin, Werner Möller

Project management
Tim Leik

Spatial and graphic design
Werner Möller, Prill Vieceli Cremers

Modelmaking
Hennig Seilkopf, Holger Ziolkowski
Chris Krause, Norman Strzelecki
Darja Deising

**Reconstruction and assembly of furniture
from the 'Volkswohnung'**
Deutsche Werkstätten Hellerau GmbH:
Tobias Kandt, Thomas Redweik, Anette Hellmuth
und die Lehrlinge: Hermine Gerber, Alexandra
Kloppe, Manfred Müller, Johannes Oehme, Josef
Schuppe, Eric Schuster

and the Arbeits- und Sozialförderungsgesellschaft
Dessau e.V.:
Lothar Lubitzsch, Frank Lüer

Restoration supervisor
Frank Ardelt

Construction and installation of exhibition elements
Pollmer GmbH, design by Rainer Zahrend, CDT
advertising and printing by Dimitri Reibestein,
Hilmar Prüß, Jan Steinbrück

Digital image processing
Anne Meyer

Copy editors
Karola Handwerker Heinze,
Katrin Globke, Benita Weise

Translations
Rebecca Philipps Williams, George Wolter,
Katrin Globke

Public relations
EINSATEAM, Eidner & Merker GbR, Berlin
Jutta Stein, Tassilo Constantin Speler

Mediation "Junge Werkstatt"
Leon Claus

**With special thanks to the following for their
assistance:**
Philipp Potocki, Daniel Weiss, Inge Wolf, Astrid
Volpert, Anke Blümm, Vincent Grünthal, Ulrich
Nickmann and all those involved from the
collective of the Bauhaus Dessau Foundation

Loans

Originals:
gta Archives / ETH Zurich
Kunstmuseum Olten
Siedlungsgenossenschaft Freidorf, Muttenz

Digital images:
Deutsches Architekturmuseum, Frankfurt
gta Archive / ETH Zurich
Bauhaus-Archiv, Berlin
Schusev State Museum of Architecture, Moscow
Siedlungsgenossenschaft Freidorf, Muttenz
Archiv der Moderne, Bauhaus-Universität Weimar
Zentrum Paul Klee, Bern
Staatsarchiv, Basel-Stadt
Stadtarchiv, Dessau-Roßlau
Federal Archives, Coblenz
Yael Aloni, Sharon Archive, Tel Aviv

Peter Glöckchen Wendy John

NEVER is an awfully long time!

Collective 38

Frodo
Sam
Merry
Pippin
Gandalf
Aragorn
Boromir
Legolas
Gimli

Help!

Collective 39